The Defective Model

I0104000

AJ Romano

chipmunkapublishing

the mental health publisher

Published by

Chipmunkapublishing

PO Box 6872

Brentwood

Essex CM13 1ZT

United Kingdom

http://www.chipmunkapublishing.com

Copyright © AJ Romano 2011

Edited by Mirela Zotinca

Chipmunkapublishing gratefully acknowledge the support of Arts Council England.

"People are strange, when you're a stranger…no one remembers your name, when you're strange…"
- Jim Morrison and The Doors

AJ Romano

About the Author

AJ Romano, born June 8th, 1988, grew up and currently resides in the state of NJ, about twenty-miles south of New York City. AJ has had to cope with various mental health diagnosis' throughout his twenty-two years including Bipolar Disorder, Clinical Depression, General Anxiety Disorder, and most frequently Panic Disorder. He has been writing poetry to help cope with his emotions for "as long as he knew how to write". He is currently finishing his Bachelors of the Arts in English with the University of Phoenix, with aspirations of continuing his education with a Masters of the Fine Arts Degree in Creative Writing. His goal, as of now, is to obtain a college-level teaching position, while continuing to compose his work. Unfortunately, psychological conditions are hard to treat and impossible to cure, and AJ's story is ongoing. "Poetry", he states, "will always be my therapy."

AJ Romano

Dedicated to my Old Man, Mommy, Mike, and Ryan.

I always had you guys, even if I didn't know it.

AJ Romano

Table of Contents

AJ Romano

Disclaimer

Spring-cleaning for a writer such as myself, an *emotional* writer, really only has one comparison; a flower that continues to renew itself, year after year, until it becomes so regular its beauty is ignored. I have always written to cope; whether poetry, prose, journal entries, or lines on scrap pieces of paper. That being said, writing this book became more *revision* than *writing* in and of itself. The entries in this book are not written in the past tense and certainly not "sugar-coated"; this is a real account of my life as it was happening. There are certainly "reflective" poems, but "reflection" is a relative term. Those poems were written not a year later, six-months later, or even really a month later. My personal thoughts on page, reflecting my personal life, have taken flight.

I have suffered for most of my life. I know more about night than dreary day because something (anxiety, depression, mania or what have you) has always been there to keep me staring at the ceiling, knowing that responsibility is a few hours away. The result is a hangover it takes days to sleep off.

I could give you a laundry-list of medications the professionals with good intentions, *their* good intentions, have given me, recommended to me, and gave me ultimatums to take. I am not deaf anymore to the countless others like me. I was a slave to pills; an addict without an addiction, an addict to cyclical self-medication, and finally an addict with an addiction. Being brutally honest, to me, as needed meant *exactly that*.

In retrospect, my self-medication was probably problematic, and I am NOT talking about marijuana. I put pot in the same category as Valium; a short-term fast-acting band-aid. No, I am talking about my "cyclical addictions". I was smart enough to never let one substance take control; my weeks' calendar was filled with different remedies. Bottles of Nyquil, boxes of Benadryl, anti-anxiety, pain medication, muscle relaxers, sleeping pills, and alcohol got me by, barely alive, for years.

My addiction but not-addiction ranks first on the "Fuck AJ and His Life Up" list. The still-questionable bipolar diagnosis was certain at the time. The experiences that followed were trauma for the psyche. Situations can get worse much more quickly than you would imagine; a spiral straight down an old, abandoned well with slippery walls and only a small, pinprick of light in sight. Then night falls, and the light dwindles. Letting go of the light means turning the gun on your-self. It was close.

I suppose that is where the hospitalization comes in. I try not to look at my 36-hour experience in a psychiatric ward as a negative experience, but it is difficult. Taking pills before an evaluation seems as futile as giving an AIDs patient antibiotics, and telling them to sleep it off. After not eating because "there is none left", I checked out Against Medical Advice, amid nasty stares from an extremely affronted resident. That situation, those thirty-six hours, is one of the few things I can credit for keeping me sane years later. It was course for comparison.

I fought for a years simply on the principle that I would NEVER be institutionalized again.

Outpatient care with a psychiatrist who does not give a fuck is more management than treatment. Legal drugs made life worse than the self-medicating days. I lived the life of a zombie. I could not socialize; I could not function; I could not even watch a movie without falling into oblivious half-sleep, resulting in coma-like nothingness. The commute to work or school became a never-ending battle, a hazard for my life and the life of others that happened to cross my path. The pills stopped, *against medical advice*, the day my life almost did going seventy-five on the highway.

Now what? I lied. I went so far as to fill the prescriptions so they would show up the insurance bill. The days were better, and mood more manageable on massive amounts of marijuana and the occasional Valium for drastic measures. I could function, for the most part, for a while, anyway.

The extent of my advocacy and defensive of my marijuana use stops at the long-term. It may work for some, and I am not deaf to that. For me, however, it turned its back faster than a snobby bitch if you wore brown shoes with black pants. When the remedy became my enemy, I conceded to consult the professionals. I was, however, going to do it my way this time. I was taking control, with my back against a wall.

The Valium stopped coming as well. It had become a problem. I withdrew and ceased the habit, without any steps or any God to give me twelve-steps or support groups.

Panic light attacked me multiple times a day. For weeks I would lie in bed, getting up to eat and shower; exit from my basement room for any length of time set off a symptomatic heart attack. Anxiety had taken control of my life, just like the Valium, the hospitals, and the doctors. A few Emergency Room visits later...

Therapy was terribly unappealing. Impartial as the therapist is supposed to be, you are still, in essence, paying them for their judgment. If you make a judgment, you are not impartial...do you see my dilemma? I am a stubborn person, and, at this point, my trigger finger was getting itchy. I conceded to the concept of dialogue.

My life is a work in progress. The following pages were written for me, and others like me. It took a lot to come to the realization that there *are* other people like me, and yes, they probably understand; the result of the man I speak with twice a week, every week. The result of the man who changed my life.

I cannot reiterate enough the extent that I believe this book is therapeutic. I see my life on pages and it makes my thoughts real. For me, and for years, pretending to be a dumbed down version of me I was not was a very large part of the problem. More important than being therapeutic for me, however, I want it to be therapeutic for us, in a broad sense. We know who we are, and the casual reader does as well. We are the over-thinkers, the outcasts, and the isolated. We are too busy getting lost in our minds to take part in social interaction. We are the heterosexuals without girlfriends (or that make their girlfriend's miserable), the closet-homosexuals, the picked-on, abused, forgotten, misguided, drug-addicted, disturbed, or the unloved. A diagnosis does not make a person different from any other person; a situation, or deformity, or handicap is wholly irrelevant. Do not think my situation was any worse than yours; just try to learn from it. Maybe it will catch early and changed something in someone at some pivotal life decision. Maybe someone will laugh and think "been there..."

The Defective Model

I was one of the lucky ones. I survived to tell the tale; an old (at 22 years) pirate with a peg-leg, cigar, and a bottle of rum telling battle stories. Many of us don't. The seas of the mind are treacherous and misleading. Now when I lament, I try to think of the others who do not have good health insurance and a caring family. My *mind* isolated me, but they are fucked either way. So maybe that is what this is about. Empowerment is a loaded term these days, used too loosely. I have not become empowered. I have become aware, and finally awake. I am especially aware that the fight will be never-ending. *Living* is the prize for victory.

I am not advocating any treatment, or solution. The book makes my *mind-frame* apparent to the reader, with the sole purpose of relative experience. I know that many will read this book, start to finish, and believe that it was about themselves. Do not feel isolated by the situation you are in. Others like you exist.

To the casual reader, take a look into my mind. The poems and prose enclosed, while not dated exactly, are in chronological order; the chapters in my book are the stages of my life as it has gone. This is what we really feel like. Please remember that the next time your bipolar employee calls out of work. And enjoy, I guess.

You are not alone. Find an outlet, and stick with it. The following pages were mine.

AJ Romano

Predisposition

Narcotic (2004)

Everything good,

is not good.

Illegal drugs?

No DARE, they do fucking help.

Happiness? Not.

For putting off the inevitable—

a miracle.

Jesus healed the sick,

put off pain until inevitable death.

Percocet's function is not destruction,

but miracle-making.

The Norm (10/20/04)

If you think you're sane

you are more fucked up

than the rest of us.

Untitled* (2005)

Hooked on the rush,

overwhelming, catalyzing,

the Tango of my senses.

Tasting defiance a thrill,

I store it in my filing cabinet,

for later review.

It satisfies cravings—

love, hate, and indifference;

overcomes violent impulse.

Thoughts ignore curves and bends

on the paved roads of the Dark.

Preferring the straight, rugged road,

less traveled,

death by association.

Cereal and fucking milk.

*taken from a journal entry

Sea of Glass (2006)

Sometimes I feel drowning

into a sea of glass nothingness

is a viable option;

submerge into smooth bass lines

and take short, panic breaths.

My brain intoxicates

with the flow of the current,

disguised in acoustic.

(Untitled from a piece of scrap paper, 2006)

Bland boys cry rainbows

in to glasses half-empty

while childhood mockingbirds take flight

into storms of deceit.

Winds rock boats with feather beds

and waves breach cabins bathing the Captain,

as he drinks from his flask of nobility

for the last time.

Nyquil and Xanax (2008)

Insomnia is a coma violently turned inside out. Simple tasks such as cooking or washing dishes become as arbitrary as drinking coffee. The *monotony* is the Achilles tendon, not the fact that I have been literally awake pretty much my entire life. The monotony overwhelms you, until staring at the ceiling for even one more second becomes more life threatening than dropping into a triple-threat cage match with Dahmer and the Zodiac.

The key to survival is to fill your sleepless nights with even more, ever increasingly meaningless tasks. Make excuses to take a drive to your local convenience store and pick up a nice bottle of liquid Nyquil. Knock down half the bottle before your key hits the ignition, and take the drive home. Head to the kitchen, and you will soon find yourself immersed with balloons or paper bags or some other meaningless object that, regardless of meaning, passes the time much more quickly than one would imagine.

Before you can understand the Nyquil's perspective, you must understand the effects of said Nyquil. This amazing concoction has the wonderful power of tricking your body into believing it is asleep, and thus unlocking the subconscious mind without ever hitting REM. I find marijuana has similar effects for the insomniac, yet unfortunately it is not always simply a Quickie Mart away. Medicinally I believe in the ability of THC to dissolve pain and stress simultaneously, without the addictive properties of my next paragraph.

Xanax was produced as a short-term anti-anxiety medicine. Unfortunately, however, it made its way on to the list of the top-ten prescribed medicines of 2006, in the good company of a little drug called Vicodin (or, as I prefer to call it, prescription heroin). These "short-term" drugs are being used as long-term treatments, and, eventually the user (or abuser) builds a tolerance. A gentleman of a weaker mind than my own may allow this to lead to dependence. However, having "been down that road", strictly speaking I cheated and read the ending. Because, what happens when these "licensed drug dealers" decide enough is enough? You end up on the streets, scoring the white powder just to get through the day.

The day a substance controls me is the day you can write me a prescription for a 9mm and a bottle of Jameson so I can blow my fucking brains right out of my head.

So I choose to suffer. I choose to stare at the somewhat empty bottles of Soma, Klonopin, Elavil, and Buspar on my dresser. I choose to not refill my happiness pills that would inevitably choke and sputter the ever-loving life out of me.

I lie in bed, frustrated with myself. Is it my fault I am a "defective model"? I lie in bed frustrated with healthcare, knowing my next step is the inevitable addiction; all the while juggling my job and its worth on a scale next to marijuana and well being.

I resolve it within me and down half a bottle as the key pierces the ignition, aware that I am moving toward a white, padded room of inevitability, praying that something will spare my pain for even a second; hoping that tonight, maybe tonight, I will enjoy the joy of true conscious escape. It's just some food for thought.

(Untitled from another piece of scrap paper, 2008)

Pardon the appearance.

I am just a degenerate, to a conservative society,

overcome with emotions.

My eyes well with joy

from the smoke in my eye,

and the Jack on my breath.

Please, continue.

Streaks of Gold Drugs... (2007-8)

Streaks of gold line the path well crossed

and, trust me, well trodden

and very versed in many pairs of feet.

The road forks and, rather than the treacherous gold,

I choose the conservative pen.

"Nothing gold can stay..."

Sweet Peaches and Jagged Cliffs (titled 2011, written 2008)

October air expands and contracts happiness

through tubes of hate

and eases rugged minds

over terrain of past mistakes

and past betrayals

and falling from jagged cliffs.

White foam and straight seas,

weather-beaten sails

and weather-beaten sailors,

smelling of stale whiskey and sweet tobacco

prepare for a soft land-fall.

They leave behind the swash-buckling life

for nameless sunsets, sweet peaches,

and a fair trade wind,

pointing North from rock-bottom,

with a broken compass and backwards map.

Before Color TV (A Reflection on the Beginning)

Warm thoughts,

chilled by thrill and let down—

destroyed by doubt.

Waking hours play games,

volatile energy in the moon craters

marking my mind;

reception results

in rapid ascension

to God's perfection.

Rejection rips thought,

a numbing I never felt coming.

Before color TV's turned on,

was everyone doomed

to brood in black and white?

Bipolar Blues

Perception

Titled poetry—

titled life.

Definition of haves and have-nots,

do and done,

inherited and earned,

use and abuse.

Blurry bar-room bleakness

turns titles to PhD's

because loose women are like loose change,

meaningful with a heavy pocket

but easily forgotten when you drop a penny.

I may as well title every poem *That Bipolar Kid*.

The Blind Squirrel...

It hurts most to see abstract color

in simple black and white,

sailing down a round hallway

closing in on myself.

The hallway widens and widens;

widening, until north becomes east,

confusing most calibrated compasses;

mine was decomposed from overuse.

Direction seems clownish—

blinded by black and white.

The Eternal Optimist

Assimilation, I would say, is the hardest part.

Knowing they know,

but fall into an abyss of ignorance

kicks me in the shins harder

than Douche ever did in 4th grade;

(did I know then?)

How do you feel?

My favorite question's disposition: the glass is half empty.

You can't medicate wit.

Any Number of Days

Living pill to pill in college

is sitting down for hours on end,

for ceaseless hours,

until your legs go numb

and you are too weak to hold your body weight,

much less quicken the pace.

Prescriptions place you in outer-space,

off the charts of the physical plane

and beyond the scope of the cosmos

and not inter-dimensional, or dimensional,

but *non-dimensional*.

dead on the inside and out.

I should have gotten a DUI for doing it *their* way:

"Sir, are you under the influence of any drugs or alcohol?"

"Officer, do you have cable television? Have you ever listened to the side-effects in an Abilify commercial?"

Jingle Jangle

I heard Mr. Poe's Bells,

jingling

jingling

jingling

calling the voice spinning brain neurons or something,

but it resonates, you know?,

especially when logic behind the act

tips the scale to stark reality;

I am alone.

Hans Solo

That's kind of what fuels heaven and Hell;

indecision as indecisive

as doubling-down

when your luck is down:

"Give it one more shot...",

The card flipped at that moment,

that very moment, adrenaline rising

before inevitably falling—

Niagra in a barrel.

You wake up without coffee and Heaven consumes you

with all its blessings,

flip a new card, and bust again.

It doesn't matter really;

Hell missed me.

I missed him, too.

When you live in hyperspace,

monotony gets boring.

St. Peters University Medical Center

Embarrassment is the only emotion I remember,

I think; the look on their faces—

the realization this blur or blip

in a life-span's radar

would lead to Hiroshima.

I reflected later, alone,

after the Ativan shot, of course;

contemplating selfishness

from a hospital bed.

I didn't look in the mirror the next morning.

Hospitalized

It didn't seem real at first in all honesty;

coherence eventually registered my self-image.

Degraded,

cold drafts swept up

my night-before hospital gown on the *bench of insanity*.

They called it "patient registration".

I took in the zombies for what they were—

rendered unconscious by Medical Capitalism;

staff lunches and Yankee tickets for prescriptions.

The more the better.

They? "We" is a better word choice.

I took in the zombies for what *we* were,

and what we used to be.

What they made us.

The Empty Shells

I'm pretty sure I lost some of my soul that night.

I was conned.

"This will help you sleep"

translated to: "This will make you manageable."

I was alluded by the "lingo".

They gave us a few extra minutes of television

after our late-night cigarette for the Celtics/Lakers game.

I hate basketball.

Foiled against the roaring,

raging, rampant crowd immersed in one constant,

joyous and celebratory occasion,

we were dead inside ourselves.

Do pills drive you to insanity,

or does insanity drive you to pills,

and, by the way,

the chicken or the egg?

Soul-Robbers with Degrees

Either way, it's fucked really.

It must be easy, self-deprecating too,

sit behind a desk with a pen and blue pad comparing lives:

Hallucinations or mania,

panic disorder, psychosis, or depression,

addiction—

more prescriptions.

Oh, that's right. The bill.

I'll write you a check.

Hitler thought he was right too,

he just didn't *charge* the Jews for their souls.

AJ Romano

Routines of the Mentally Diseased

Every day I eat

one of these, once a day,

one of those, twice a day,

and one of those, once a day

for a week until your body gets a tolerance

then take it twice a day for two weeks

then we meet again and I charge you

to give you more pills that other doctors say work

so they must (right?).

I remember third grade or something

the letters DARE meant something.

They taught us about dependency.

After a few years smoking pot,

masking your face for the mirror—

teaches tolerance.

Thanks, I'll save a trip to the pharmacy.

A mask is a mask.

Humor Me

Doctors direct the dichotomy between "use" and "abuse";

a job that should clearly be left to the user and abuser.

Everything is rated on a scale of one to ten.

Recurring symptoms worsen symptoms.

The use of a scale with a peak,

asymptomatic.

When a paranoid

anxiety-ridden

depression-plagued

mania-addicted

self-medicating

bipolar psychiatrist

tells me what to take and when to take it,

I'll eat this poem.

The Defective Model

Until then, I guess I'll just write more poems

I won't end up eating.

The Last Day I Took Those Fuckers

White lines zipped away thoughts at 2pm—

I had class at 3.

Nine-hours lying in the void of half-sleep,

half-drugged-coma was ill-sufficient

to overcome prescription power.

I fell hard.

Jolted to semi-consciousness, I touched the brake;

the rumble strip a smooth, Shakespearean sonnet

of death-preventing proportion.

The nearly wrecked innocence of the gentlemen in the lane beside me

was clearly expressed by the blast of his horn and the gesture he offered.

I reclined my seat and nature took hold on the side of a major highway.

Dead to the world.

Self-Medication

There it is, you see,

bliss of half-sleep,

comatose and blank,

dead to the world.

The world dies too,

largely the point.

I drank until I never came down—

drunk with mania,

I needed to drink to sleep

and I knew and I saw

my mind and my body deteriorating;

I was watching my life,

the mirror after a steaming shower;

a medical or genetic or degenerate mistake;

becoming another statistic with a sponsor.

AJ Romano

And that's how I became immune to hang-overs.

I moved home next semester.

Another location, another remedy.

Into the Void

An Ode to Diazepam

Trapped living is not living.

I knew you once, you know.

I trusted you.

I had a leaning-post to keep me breathing

and free.

Unmentionable death is lonely.

Isolated. Wanting.

Requiring.

Now, a black, boarded up box with no windows.

I once "followed the drinking gourd"

and your path to freedom.

They guided me on a railroad

out of my mind.

Our Siamese-bond was effective,

and a little dab will do ya'.

The calms comes

stoning to death doubt, regret,

distress when I dream at night.

There is no fight in the dream,

but an elegant dance

with a blue beauty named Valium,

and she always invites me in after.

Better, and Medication-Free, Days

Relative

It was on me before I could breathe,

much less defend myself.

Ripping and tearing and shredding my flesh

I was nothing

my existence was nothing

and all I could think was whether

I would be remembered as nothing,

lying there—

a vulnerable puppy the first time off the tit.

.

My vulnerability was revealing.

My lack of control, ironic.

One last act of desperation,

one last chance to imagine redemption

when the pain ended as quickly as it had begun—

a sharper aftermath.

It was dead, I was broken.

Not victory, Social Darwinism.

Yeah, it kinda feels like that.

Conscious for Subconscious

I had a dream last night.

I never thought I would see her again;

let her inflict cardiac damage again.

Rage-panic-betrayal-negative-esteem disorder.

Can I be cured, doc?

Existence exercises itself,

once a day, every day, for twenty minutes;

while dieting, the best-case scenario.

They laughed.

"You can have him," she said,

in a clever ruse that was all on me, I'm sure.

I got up that morning, after awhile.

Expectations (Perception is Reality...?)

Dreams foreshadow a day doused in sunlight and drenched in rain;

downpours of pain clouding sight,

making travel hazardous, at the least.

A Floridian shower is expected,

yet frowned upon none the less.

They know the sun will return it's glory,

boasting brilliance to the vacant storm.

Sometimes I do, too.

An Attempt at Companionship

I get confused sometimes,

when I think of them at the same time.

Am I hanging on to threads never woven,

or is she terrified at the thought of me.

What could have been?

Is my delusion reflecting—

mirror, mirror, on the wall

who *is* the most tragic one of all?

I may be the lucky one though,

having another life on my conscious,

an unbearable burden.

Mesothelioma and Blindness

Are babies scolded when they fall and fall,

before, in that anticipatory moment of parenthood,

take that first step?

The step to preschool and bagged lunches,

middle school

and pivotal life choices,

high school and flammability;

adulthood, and more flammability;

you'll burst flame—

Triangle Shirtwaist.

Sometimes you can braille your way to the safety

and cancer, of asbestos.

Procrastination for survival.

Campbell's

Death is wholesome, you know?

A glass of milk that fills you up in between meals

but never really fills you up.

Ignorance over sustainability.

A fucking Ritz cracker

swimming in a sea of over-salted mushroom soup.

Four beers *clink* shrewdly in a still night,

filling the void until tomorrow;

a new day, a new remedy,

a new memory, and a new defeat.

I think I can, I think I can, I think I can...

Matchsticks Metaphor

It was fair to consider us suburban terrorists.

I think I could teach the IRA a few things about bomb-making.

Lets fill a thirty-two ounce Gatorade bottle—

match stick heads,

taped strikers on the inside,

sealed with ten rolls of electrical tape,

throw it, and let Nature take its course.

Carrying it to Ground Zero that night;

we could have died that night,

if one wrong move

struck one wrong match head

the wrong way causing a chain-reaction

resonating for miles,

raining flaming match-heads

and concussion propulsion

with murderous intent on its architects.

Volatile: that's the word.

Smoking Kills, Slower Anyway

I felt guilty, at first, wasting money—

toilet paper prescriptions for a member of MADD

at a high-school grad party.

Someone somewhere sometime said

"Perception is reality".

Other than Murphy, that's the best advice I've gotten

since Mom told me not to smoke,

lighting another herbal Xanax.

I felt guilty every time they asked.

Sure, one of these twice a day,

and one of those, and those?

No, just once a day.

I'm not placing blame.

I'm doing a pack a day.

Panic-Stricken to Cobain's Shotgun

Solitude

Every day when dawn draws I look for love

within my mind.

I wake with earthquakes

no scale could scale,

if adequate scale existed.

I mourn mornings these mornings, dread daylight
death—

the conformity everyone craves at my expense.

I smile, sometimes;

for them, at least.

Inside is impending death, though.

AJ Romano

Tidal Overflow

I feel as you feel—

I feel for you and against you,

with you or without you.

I feel feelings

seeping endless emotion

over-flowing my flood-plain.

It is a flood-plain, and it floods.

Where do the waters go when there is nowhere left

and the rains persist

and persist

and WILL NOT STOP

until Mardi Gras takes place in Atlantis?

Pocket Aces

Bleak cancer-ridden lives

rival filled-chemotherapy half-lives—

an unanswered letter without return address

may expect a response, too.

Sometimes we settle to masquerade,

because regardless of ethics,

showing the ace in your sleeve is never prudent;

busted or not.

Light Speed

How could I forget palm-sweat

and craving oxygen, chest caving in,

thoughts drifting by with cries

of motion-sickness at different times?

And the same time.

Don't you think I remember dying every day?

I pay that price to survive;

numbing

palpitating

disorienting

and surreal as it is.

I try to "think happy thoughts"—

barely even echoing at the speed of light.

The Boy Who Cried Wolf

Help propels bullets—

black powder for insatiable and maddening
puzzle-pieces paranoia-fitted over-logically.

My analysis unlocks the hallway leading no place.

At the end stands a Stepfordized me,
free from bondage, and nothing more.

His emotional ranged skewed,
he remains plateaued;
sometimes I at least get on a ski-lift.

A cruel insult to intelligence,
and nothing more.

Transformation

Ties between tides blind bonds—

day and night,

conscious and sub-conscious,

id and superego.

In sleep-movies I make the traps.

Watch the Psychiatric resident have a panic attack!

Get addicted to Valium, or submit to a bed-ridden existence!

What fun! So much fun,

it may warrant nine-or-so bloody sequels.

I'm sure the mirror would reveal darkness behind my eyes

if ever I looked in one.

The Defective Model

December 7th, 2010

Activism is the illusion of choice.

Reading tea-leaves with anticipation?

The slot machine will pay-out eventually,

and twelve hand-washes a day will prevent swine flu.

We love to combine reason and fate;

I think the Greeks left us that.

Instilled beliefs and megalomania

rarely result in suspense.

Take control of your life!

But you don't understand,

its not me,

it's the me hanging from a noose on our old bunk-beds;

he has been there for years.

AJ Romano

Poor Fucking Me

Should I just cry?
Or do I try to cope with the ball
in the back of my throat,

and slow-down, and lift-off—
a blood-hound out for blood.

I kick the closed-door open and expect
to find more than poor fucking me
moping and groping and hoping
for something more.

I do cry, on occasion.

Sanctuary

Hiding from yourself for most of your life

fakes grandeur,

makes difference,

and *effects* opinion.

Feeding off feelings

and feeling off emotions

demeans love and life

and demonizes those you love,

and those in your life.

Movies are wonderful; escaping reality—

someone else's problems for two hours.

When I Was a Kid

Fun House mirror-rooms introduce children to self-loathing.

Expecting to guess around

every tight, compact corridor is meant for suspense:

finds indicate human improvement.

Realizing the only thing stalking your "life"

around every tight, compact corner is your life,

is progression by way of acceptance.

Tall, skinny,

short, fat,

or *distorted*; all irrelevant.

We will become what we will be.

To the trained eye, that isn't so Fun.

On the Real

The real is really wrong.

Delusions of mental strength—

a new mother dead on the table may be blissful,

but she is still dead.

Her newborn lives to see tomorrow,

and her ABC's and 1-2-3's,

and Junior High,

and High School,

and maybe even University X

all the while knowing its life

killed its creator.

Hell of a concept.

Enough is Enough

Dawn balls up and stretches,

ready for a wretched fight that might

result in a tumult of temperature

decline: defining ice-memories.

I watch the pieces stop dropping at exhaustion--

no more remain.

Burrowing holes like evil moles,

destruction is their function.

The muddied floor slowly reveals

memories blocked with age,

tapped with rage;

suppression suppresses

depression and tension;

prolonging the tragic song

until one flies over the cuckoos nest

and its medication time again.

If I had any.

Unreachable

I don't know if delusion

or manic propulsion

gave me the assumption

that I could defy gravity.

It seems to teem with irrelevance.

Up I went, care-free and careless,

running rapid like a rabbit on acid;

creating grandeur might as well be cancer,

a cataclysm registering on Richter.

Fail. Failure. Failed.

I won't leave a forwarding address.

The Scars

Love leaves marks—

Leave love?

Love leaves me here.

I live to give,

I live for love,

I live for others love.

I have none of my own.

My scars have disappeared,

clear as stained glass;

getting more transparent by the second.

Vibrant as mother-fucking Technicolor.

To die! To sleep!

Selfish, for my sake.

The Forever Limbo

Its time to forget the let-down drowning pride

before it breaks your stride.

I'll be gone, Mom.

I'll be dead, Dad.

I can't fight, Mike; though I owe you that.

It's the tortoise and the hare,

and somebody flipped my ass over.

Move on, I'll take you with me.

Simply Suicide

Grief and relief

stop tingling extremities

and inflate my deflated lungs

and slow my droning heart

and make my mind comply,

moving and soothing as slowly as possible,

relishing the best seconds of my life,

before there is no more flash in my eye

or slice of my tongue,

and I lie at peace.

Yes, that kind of relief.

A Flash of Life

Calm passing over a shivering spine

finds its way to the mind releasing puzzle pieces;

painted pictures on Mom's hallway wall

illustrating innocent crimes we used to pass the time,

snippets of crickets chirping,

watching smoke rise above heads

with glassy eyes,

brothers and neighbors fighting

over this ball or that ball,

the fluid and elusive bath-tub waterslide,

and the full-contact basement brawls

me and Mike called hockey games.

Until mental tyranny takes control,

and glassy eyes turn empty and tragic.

Will my soul remain?

AJ Romano

Gray-Area

My Secular God-Send

A man with a plan.

He knew what he started.

Chain-reaction triggered

insolence, apparent from the start,

makes MD look vague

and rather unappealing.

Prescriptions equal dollar signs,

and, seriously, Plato was right;

dialogue is priceless

(whether Socrates was real, or not).

How long have you been feeling this way?

Well, AJ (he cares enough to remember my nickname?)

I am not convinced you are Bipolar at all.

Wait, WHAT?

I do not think I have ever skipped before.

Wrong, or Simply Misguided?

(Psychotherapy Phase)

Back to Perception

The issue of trust—

ignorance really is bliss,

and yet I've not been blessed.

Pretend, Pretend, Pretend.

He must have seen the tan-lines

where the mask meets my hair line.

Having much practice acting,

I know a bluff when I see one,

and he was genuine.

Someone *knows* me.

I released the chain and threw open the door,

inviting him in for a beer, and a fat Cuban.

AJ Romano

He Had Me At…

Why this is happening

happening to you

you, alone, isolated

different,

not necessarily unique

why you can't get out of bed

why you have heart attacks

why you have strokes

why you live in dreams

why you can't hold down a job or relationship

why you are fucking Lancelot at King Panic's round
table,

head-knight in a Crusade with yourself

a Grail-quest for complacency.

Newton's Third works both ways, I think.

Slow Torture

Dialogue, again, its dialogue--

unlocking passageways to caves

unbeknownst to all but Freud.

Chemical band-aids are plagues

in and of themselves,

ravishing you and all that is *you*.

So you search for yourself

in the void now containing

an empty shell of your former self.

It's time to reinvent,

session by session.

Until then, you might as well be pulling fingernails.

Regression for Progression

So, the solution is more pollution

for my serotonin gland.

The time to buy time and stubbornly cry

has been bed-ridden for weeks.

Book after story stops boredom—

anxiety-ridden depression progresses

and cultivates more and more

anxiety-ridden depression.

When nothing else remains

you may as well sing and dance in the rain,

hoping you will dry off, eventually.

The Lotus

When the door closes,

and that little thing that makes a weird hum to ensure privacy outside the door

turns on,

I breathe easy. Clarity takes hold.

Information, he says, is key.

A change in (that word again) perception.

Impartial is never impartial without intelligence,

and introspection.

Experience too, I think.

Mom, Dad, I saw Jesus today;

feet on the desk and coffee in hand.

Enlightenment is clarity.

Acceptance for Acceptance's Sake

The Truth-Mirror

Was it in a dream,

buried in whispers, that we've met?

I can't be sure if the ominous figure

(painted by the Sun on the oil-stained canvas)

who stalks silently behind me is surreal illusion,

invisible to sense.

I feel the silent stalking and whispers

resonating decibels

no ear could decipher.

They are ghosts of whispers:

of childhood innocence and untapped potential

and nonchalance,

of gluttony and sloth and five others,

and nonchalance.

The Defective Model

I sculpt my face to embody a surprise ruined from the start,

staring into reflective sarcasm.

Truth costs five dollars in the Home and Garden section,

unless that little yellow ball with the John Wayne hat

"rolls it back".

Me, Myself, and I

My groggy eyes take in my basement room for the first
time of the day—

it remains unchanged.

This is the moment I make the most pivotal decision of
the day.

Do I get up?

My silenced cell phone says 1 pm when

I check text messages and missed calls—

society never came calling.

My head is San Andreas

and my stomach isn't much better,

as usual. I get up and drone on.

I drone; worker-bees to slave

theories of *Better* men

for the sake of productivity,

and for me.

For a change.

AJ Romano

Constants Make the World Go 'Round

My bathroom is still pink—

the old woman who lived here six years ago now.

Dad was going to redo that bathroom

so many times on so many breaks from work

he called "vacations".

It remains unchanged,

other than the clothes I probably left on the floor.

I try to avoid straight coffee because I only drink it black,

and I broke a caffeine addiction awhile ago

but I drink it when I need it;

hustled and bustled busting ass trips to work,

knowing that I am already five minutes late.

These things remain unchanged.

The slick trick to getting through an inevitable fifteen-hour day?

Pretend it's a ten-hour day.

When you realize busting your ass and getting underpaid

The Defective Model

for ten hours is far from worth it,

you view the other five hours differently; a tipping scale.

But you rigged the scale, you still worked

fifteen hours and you are still tired;

feeling better than you did when you woke up.

You are living.

I am living.

Is This Atheist?

Structure gave birth,

science explains—

an algebraic equation for predicting snow-flake patterns.

Whitney and Ford were praised.

Revolutionizing eras!

They probably never thanked their parents.

The pieces were always there;

put the circle in the circle hole.

Plato, the grand-champion of science,

and Emerson, America's Romantic,

called Man "brutish".

Enlightenment at its finest.

Intelligence is negative intellect;

the ability to admit defeat

and chalk one up for the abstract on Nature's dartboard.

The Defective Model

Men of genius see more than primary colors.

I am a genetic mishap, and nothing less.

I am Pretty Sure This One Is…

"Natural" terms carry Atlas' weight.

(What is "natural"?)

Coming to terms?

Do not be concerned with someone's God.

Concern yourself with *yourself*.

There was no higher purpose—

inter-connected, the web of a greedy spider,

nature is not self-aware like God.

Man made God self-aware—

flipping a light-switch to cope with the "why"

rather than accepting the "what",

and the "what now".

Karma

I learned a few things in high school.

Cruelty due to difference—
I started out as Columbine's starting quarterback,

I became different.
Then I was holding the gun, pipe bomb at hand.
Did they know I was different?

Perceptions change; with it, reality.

Do we reap what we sow?
A nice thought, but relevant to progress?
The whole "why" thing, again.

The Grand Finale!

Story-time is over, folks.

I spoke of life, and the trifles of strife

accompanying zombies wherever they go.

Watching television is a gateway drug to hypochondria—

internet connection is the heroin needle.

The middle ground lies somewhere between

cries of agony and drug-dealers

with prescription pads.

Dialogue is my scripture—

if I need a pill to renew my faith from time to time,

so be it.

Moderation is the message,

and control is the path.

The Defective Model

I did it for me.

And I'll do it next time.

And the time after that.